Eccentric Beauty

Poems by
Jessica Layne Bird

AuthorHouse™
1663 Liberty Drive, Suite 200
Bloomington, IN 47403
www.authorhouse.com
Phone: 1-800-839-8640

© *2009 Jessica Layne Bird. All rights reserved.*

No part of this book may be reproduced, stored in a retrieval system, or transmitted by any means without the written permission of the author.

First published by AuthorHouse 4/1/2009

ISBN: 978-1-4389-6518-5 (sc)

Printed in the United States of America
Bloomington, Indiana

This book is printed on acid-free paper.

Insightful Murmurs

History Class

Ignorance is dangerous,
When used in place of fact,
May I remind you of the inquisitions?
And other harmful acts,

May I remind you of the Holocaust,
Or how about slavery?
It's sick that in this world,
That bigotry can be called bravery,

There are the deaths of Christ,
And of Joan of Arc,
Whether you believe in them,
Or think they're just a Lark,

There's Hiroshima and Nagasaki,
Though I'm not sure what rhymes,
But those who dropped the bombs,
Were ignorant far past their times,

Let's all remember Salem…
Though its witch hunt never quit,
Because the new witch is called "terrorist",
If you're labeled, you're in *hit,

It's sad how people hate you,
If your beige, or tan or brown,
All because some years ago,
Two towers were knocked down,

The mad-men who destroyed them,
Yes, they were all ignorant too,
Because they too believed in murder,
To prove someone is less than you,

Skin color shouldn't matter,
It's an external organ, not a definition!
And you don't see Caucasians stopped at the airport,
Because some had evil intentions!

The ignorance of people,
Seems to only broadcast hates,
And sadly those who cared to learn,
All had to suffer from these fates…

Jessica Layne Bird 2008

The Human Condition

Love is, an involuntary reaction,
To an, Un-infatuated passion,
It can, take your soul,
Control your mind,
But it isn't pretty all of the time,
It's, words of love,
And words of pain,
It can raise the sun,
Or bring forth the rain,
It takes times,
Even years,
Who can hurt you most,
Can dry your tears,
But once you get it,
It will stay with you,
In your soul,
No matter what you do,
It's beautiful, though I don't know it well,
It brings you to heaven,
Though you'd face hell…

Jessica Layne Bird 2006

The Life Unlead

A beauty of earth…
Where few will ever be,
Is a place that is found,
In what you cannot see.

A place in your mind,
Where joy is there,
A time you can find,
When your pain is unaware.

It is the place where peace is,
Where together are all the pieces,
Of,

What you don't know,
And what you can't change,
Are gone in a bliss,
So sweetly deranged,

A place to never,
Be meant to explain,
Where no one can find you…
Since you have no name.

No one is there,
You are everything,
You're going nowhere,
And nowhere has meaning.

Before you turn back,
You still look ahead,
This bliss is the place,
Of the life most unlead.

Jessica Layne Bird 2007

A Child Is Born

A child is born!
A child is born!
Nothing could ever replace it,
This child was born to be the next Hitler,
This one just another Jesus,

This child was born to give his blood,
This child was born to spill it,
This child was born to revive the world,
This child was born to help kill it,

This one will become the criminal mind,
This one the chief of police,
This child will speak the words of the angels,
This one the words of the beast,

Beginning at innocence,
Is where the evil grows,
The most destructive footsteps of our time,
Began with cute tiny toes,

Another burden is made,
Another joy is created,
This one was a wonderful choice,
This one accidentally fated,

A child is born!
A child is born!
Every single day,
This one will buy their way to heaven,
This one will become a gay,

A child is born!
A child is born!
And it doesn't really matter,
Because more and more and more will come,
To replace the future, later.

Jessica Layne Bird 2007

So Many... to Prove Wrong

There are so many who just want to see me fall,
I'll prove them all wrong; I'll get it all,

I might not be as "successful" as any of them,
But money I find isn't all that comforting,

I could still be what I want to,
That's the difference between me and you,

I'll prove to myself, and you, that I can be,
More than a shell, of what I dreamed to be,

And as long as I can live,
Without hurting myself, or anybody,
What would I want with all your useless money...

Money doesn't buy happiness,
But I can agree it makes your pains,
Just a little bit less,

And I can't get this feeling out of my chest,
That I just got to do something,
Before I'm breathless,

And I don't care about anyone,
If they don't care about me,

Why should I care about,
Those who want to hurt me...

And I hope that one day,
They can all see,

That I'll get it all,
You wait and see…

Jessica Layne Bird 2003

Because You Are

Did you ever wonder why?
The darkness calls your name?
Did you ever wonder why?
You've been hunted and afraid?
Did you ever wonder why?
You never can just smile?
It seems the world won't let you?
Not even, just awhile?
Constant destruction of character,
Constant pain, and loss,
So many, yes so many,
Self proclaiming they're your boss,
Why have you been singled out?
Why you, and no one else?
The reason is because they fear you,
Because you are... yourself.

Jessica Layne Bird 2008

I'm Just another Writer, Sadly

Sadly too many people,
Will band together for hate,
Sadly all of these people,
Will be the world's fate,

Sadly too many people,
Won't stand to do what's right,
Sadly those who would have,
Fear to do much more than write,

Sadly too many people.
Don't have the means to good,
Sadly too many people,
Do nothing though they could,

Sadly we see heroism,
As a rather stupid measure,
Why help them, when I can focus,
On my own life and my own pleasures,

Why should anyone care,
Really,
"It's their life, it's not mine",
Why should anyone care,
Really,
"It will probably get better,
In time..."

Jessica Layne Bird 2008

Time

Right now,
Stop,
Look around.
See every site,
Hear every sound,
Live each day,
Each day to the fullest,
Even when times, are at their lowest,
Time stops for no man, woman or child,
So let you pain, be no more than mild,
Your strength,
Your looks,
Your faith,
Your mind,
And even your soul can wear away,
In time…

Jessica Layne Bird 2002

The Long Shot

Take the long shot,
If you don't, you'll miss,
Joys of unforeseen success,
Failures bitter-sweet kiss,

If you only take short-shots,
What's the point of life?
You'll only live once,
Don't hold back then strife,

Go for it, just go for it!
Even if you fail,
Because the failure of never trying,
Is far worse, than a lack to prevail.

Jessica Layne Bird 2008

Beautiful Situations

One Tomorrow

If someone died tomorrow,
Would anybody care,
If a child cried tomorrow,
Would you move to dry their tears,

If the world could love tomorrow,
Would you bother with today,
If the world spoke out against its wrongs,
What would you have to say,

If the whole world cried tomorrow,
For the people who lost their way,
What if the whole world,
Yes, the whole world,
Could change tomorrow today,

What if people could gather together,
And give just what they could,
To those who really had nothing,
Do you think anybody would,

What if the poets quit writing,
And went out and did what they say,
And what if tomorrow,
All the world could do the same,

What if tomorrow,
We kept every promise,
And broke all the hurtful lies,
What if tomorrow,
We gave the whole world a smile,
A day with no tearful eyes,

What if tomorrow we could stop the fight,
What if tomorrow we could all say sorry,
What if tomorrow we could be blind to color,
What if tomorrow we could see the light,
Maybe tomorrow I'll make it,

The best day of my life,
Or maybe somebody else's,
What if I could give just one person,
A little better life,

What if the fear faded tomorrow,
No one would hurt anyone,
What if for just tomorrow,
The world put down it's guns,

What if tomorrow,
Nobody died,
What if tomorrow,
No one had to cry,

What if tomorrow,
Just for one day,
The whole world could live,
In harmony for one day...

Jessica Layne Bird 2008

Angels Speak Wisdoms Unheard

Angel's lips speak wisdoms unheard,
Death and life, are decided by words,
Wealth and faith seem so intertwined,
Where the most grateful, become the unkind,

A few years later…

Tears in eyes, to show you've been hurt,
You were once taunted, used, un-alert,
But you became something by strength your mind,
But in all your glory, no joy did you find,

Nearing the end…

So you sit in you castle day after day,
Watching out windows, your life fades away,
All of it given for trinkets and bills,
And though love was lost, and the pain is there still,

It's too late…

So now you say;
"I live in this place of diamonds and lace, but everything here is
    cheap.
In luxurious comfort, is my misery,
For I left what I needed to keep."

Jessica Layne Bird 2007

After all...

Where are you now?
You who broke my heart,
Where did you run to,
The one who was so smart,

Where are you now?
You who had to flee,
Where did you fall to,
After you took all of me,

Where did the love go,
When you said it'd never end,
Where are you when I need you most,
My love, and once, my friend.

Jessica Layne Bird 2008

Nothing, Never, No one

There is nothing, nothing!
For you here,
Leave this place,
Get out!

There is nothing,
Nothing, for you to fear,
Except for your own doubt,

Don't doubt yourself,
My dear,
Please don't,
For it will trap you here forever,

Follow your dreams,
Your heart,
Your soul,
And don't you ever say never…

Jessica Layne Bird 2008

May We All Die Young

May we all die young,
May we never grow old,
May we leave this world,
Before we start to mold,

Life is not measured in days,
But how those days are measured,
In the quality not the quantity,
Of our many joys, and pleasures,

May we all be able to walk,
Until we walk with Him,
May we all be able to see,
Before the lights go dim,

May we all die young,
Young in mind and body,
May we live our lives for good,
With a touch of the harmless naughty,

May we all die young I ask,
May no one have to suffer,
And may we all see life,
As more than just a buffer.

Jessica Layne Bird 2007

In The Ruins of My Broken Heart

I feel a sadness inside me,
In the ruins of my broken heart,
A sadness… I cannot control,
It's been there from the start,

A waterfall of tears,
An ocean forms my sorrow,
A sadness killing me,
And stealing my tomorrow,

A sadness killing me,
Yet saving me from hell,
In the ruins of my broken heart,
The voices so vainly yell,

In the ruins of my heart,
So dust clouded and gray,
My empire so quickly fallen,
There was not even time to pray.

Jessica Layne Bird 2008

A Real Love Story

Will my life shine?
Or will it soon shine out,
Tears are a memory,
I'll never live without...

    ***

I miss you so, my darling,
From when we were so young,
I remember your face,
From when our love,
Had finally just begun...

We went to the carnival,
It was in town that day,
I remember biking to your door,
Your white house by the bay,

And you had a flower pinned to your hair,
Your dress a milky white,
Oh, all the butterflies,
I knew I'd have to fight,
That night...

Your jewelry it was,
Oh yes, Sarah Coventry,
And even on that very first date,
You meant so much to me...

    ***

We rode the rides of life,
The ups and downs until...
We hit a few bumps in the road,
Some pot-holes we had to fill,

Until there were no more games,
I knew what I wanted out of life,
So I got down on my once good knee,
And I made you, my wife,

I remember watching you,
Coming down the aisle,
Shining like the moon,
Your perfect virgin smile,

The way you looked that night,
You hooked me by your sight,
The night that those butterflies,
Finally won the fight...

***

And our new first borns,
They grew up oh, so fast,
But when you think about it,
As did all the years that came, and past,

And when they found loves,
Of their very own,
They all left our nesting place,
And made their own homes,

And we'd never thought we would be alone,
Again... sometimes...

***

And now today,
I sit, in my bed-side chair,
My dear you've changed,
But you're still so gorgeous,
I can't help but stare,

Your voice was like wind chimes,
Sharp and rich like the best wine,
Now poorly reduced to,
Sad, and very sickly whines,

And then you say to me,
"Hunny, I'll be fine,
And, "We've already spent,
So much wonderful time,"

It's not enough,
No it's not,
I said forever,
And that's just what I want!

"It's alright,"
"I'm not afraid,"
You whispered to me softly,
The day before you faded away,
Just ever so roughly…

***

I wore my best suit to the service that day,
How you told me?
Yes, it went exactly that way,

There were white roses to cover the ground,
And all of our old friends,
Filled up most of the crowd….

Yes, I managed to walk up,
To the top of that hill,
Where I freed you spirit,
Near the white house, by the bay, and the mill...

       ***

So now I sit,
On our old brass bed,
Decades of memories,
Fill each inch of my head,

And I thank you, dear,
For this life we've lead,
And for all of those beautiful things,
That you said.

Thank you, my darling,
My beloved wife,
You were the most precious thing,
That there was, in this old man's life...

Love S.

Jessica Layne Bird 2008

Why...

Death has become me,
I'll see no more dawn,
The same will be you to,
Too soon, before long,

Please never love me,
For I'll steal it all,
For when the day breaks,
We will finally fall,

I can't bring you with me,
And if I could, I wouldn't,
For there's so many things,
Too miss, for me...
In your life, you shouldn't,

My time is over,
My dear romance...
I think... I love you...
And for all,
Of my now found faith,
I'll soon watch from above you...

It's amazing how,
The pains of life can,
Bring out the true strengths,
Of a woman or a man,

And you're asking me, "Why now?"
I just don't have an answer,
Too soon, for us; almost lovers...
This sickness... this cancer...

Jessica Layne Bird 2008

My Soul Remembers

I remember you my love,
The one I've never seen,
I remember who you are,
The one from one life's scene,

I remember you, my dear,
Though your face evades my mind,
I remember you my lover,
The one from once lost time,

I remember you somehow,
Not your face, nor your name,
But I remember you were there somehow,
How time it was to blame,

I'll miss you now,
Forever,
And though we've never meet,
I know my soul remembers you,
The one, I can't forget.

Jessica Layne Bird 2009

Your Little Faith in Me

And so I awaken from my deceiving dreams,
And you're no longer there…
For many years it seems,

But it hasn't been that long,
Since you have been gone,
And though I wasn't always there,
It's you, who makes me strong,

So take back your faith,
Your little faith in me,
And I will stand by you,
I promise, you will see,

That I will always be there,
As much, as I can be….

Jessica Layne Bird 2008

What if?

You used to, get me so high,
But it's fleeting like a drug,
And I wonder who could love you more,
More than I could love,

And what if they could love you more,
Maybe even better,
Someone who'd give you all your dreams,
Be the warmth in our cold weather,

What if as I complain,
They'd love you as you are,
And as I searched for whom I am,
You'd find yourself a brighter star,

I want someone to catch you,
For too far have we slid,
And I am oh so sorry,
For all the things I did,

What I'm about to say,
Is not a prank or kid…

I just don't love you anymore,
But I swear,
I did…

Jessica Layne Bird 2008

Any Life to Me

My love, my darling, come lay down beside me,
Hold me close this night; to guard and to hide me,
You are the only, to give any life to me,
I'd die without you,
Or live forever lonely,

I woke up this morning, just to read the news,
I fell to the floor, as I read about you,
How could this happen to you my love?
Open your eyes, dear, for they are so beautiful,

Oh my dear God, how can this be?
I knew that you never wanted to leave,
Oh my dear God, where is he now,
What have you done with my guardian angel?

Jessica Layne Bird 2008

Any Life to You

I never told you, what you truly meant to me,
I would have sold my own soul,
Just for you to be me,
My guardian angel, I still feel your soul,
How can I listen?
How can I let you go?

What will I do when I'm soon old and gray?
And I am still longing for your youthful face?
What will I do?
What? When they tell me,
It's not the end of the world…

I'd die to be with you,
Just one last embrace,
I'd give up this world,
For your loving face,
Marry me, is what you said when you left that night,
Barry me, my love, I'll find you, soon in the light.

Jessica Layne Bird 2008

And I Just Love You More (Sadly)

I can't tell you, how I feel,
I care too much to hurt you,
But what you do, it hurts me,
And you don't even try to,

Do you know how I feel inside?
And do you really know, how,
I felt when all of my dreams died.
And how it still stings now,

You have everything in your life; you need,
But all I have is you,
And maybe that's the reason why,
I've forgiven you,

The part of me that loves you,
Is the part of me I hate,
Because it's the only part of me,
I can't, but I should shake,

Because you're just so flaw-less,
You make me feel, down and poor,
But it's because of what you are,
I can't help but love you more.

Jessica Layne Bird 2007

You Don't Know

I think you're so perfect,
Then I realize you're not,
I think you're so perfect,
Because you're all that I've got,

My life is over now,
So please leave me alone,
My life is over now,
Just go be on your own,

You and I are nothing,
Alike; you and I,
You light up our world,
My darkness makes it die,

I'm sick of loving you,
But sadly,
Yes… I do,
Because I know that someone,
Like you is very few,

But I am still alone here,
Even when I'm in your arms,
Because you don't know,
Oh you, don't know!
How it feels when your life, is gone.

Jessica Layne Bird 2006

Super-Humanism

I've watched over you for years,
I must go, it isn't safe here,
I can no longer blind your eyes,
Or keep you from the world's fear,

You are different my child,
You were born to be,
And through the harshness of this world,
You'll be forced to see,

Do not cover your face,
Do not let it be touched by tears,
For you are meant for so much more,
Than what is offered here,

Leave this place my child,
Leave and don't look back,
For one day your name will show the world,
What it before, lacked,

You may not understand this,
But give it time... you will,
And we pray you make the right choice,
For none, but you; can...
Or will...

Jessica Layne Bird 2008

Eccentric Beauty

I saw an eccentric beauty,
That beauty smiled at me,
So odd in all her grandeur,
The jester, and the queen,

So carefree in her worry,
And so awkwardly of grace,
Slower than the world,
Though she moved with quicker pace,

She looked me up and down,
As she slowly strolled the floor,
All eyes were set upon her,
Glaring, yet wishing more,

Her clothes made a quiet statement,
Blacker than the night,
Though peaceful as a fallen leaf,
They emphasized her might,

Her hand it fell upon me,
As she spoke a word or two,
She spoke to me the things,
In which I once, never knew,

A genius was this beauty,
So put together, yet so strewn,
The sanest words I'd ever heard,
As spoken from a loon.

Jessica Layne Bird 2008

The Thin Line Between Eccentrics and Truth

My Seraphic Hypocrite

You stand beside faith
Dressed in white to show your cross,
You are blind to all hate,
First to tell all, they are wrong,

You can hide who you are,
Be the first, to cast the stone,
But we see into your shadow,
Judge not: what you don't know,

So why not close your eyes,
And ignore all of your wrongs
For you know we can't,
See who you really are,

So you stand and hide,
Tell the "sinners" they should fear,
But we all know that you,
Are the only problem here,

You cast the first stone,
Blind to sins yourself commit,
We have a name for you,
My Seraphic Hypocrite,

So arm yourself with words of shame,
And drug yourself on God,
But one day you'll wake to find,
We see through your façade.

Jessica Layne Bird 2006

Ignorance

Why do all the good people die?
Why do all the bad live so long?
Why are there so few of intellect?
Why are there so many,
Who are so wrong?

The "smart" ones won't procreate,
What child deserves this life, this fate?
While the ignorant violate,
Over pro-create, and over-mate,

Just to teach their subject children,
More hate, and depravity,
While most blame the parents,
They blame society,

Of course it's society,
Of course it is,
Because in simile, it's as clean,
And as deep,
As a puddle of piss!

It's not our fault though,
No it truly isn't,
Because not knowing is not stupidity,
It's innocently,
Ignorance.

Jessica Layne Bird 2008

I Don't Care... B.S.

There are just a few things that people shouldn't care about,
But most of these things equal,
What no one will butt-out about,

Things like harmless lifestyles,
And the beliefs of others,
Or even the young women,
Who are accidental mothers,

Sex is glorified by all,
But the glares come when they keep it,
And ironically the glaring,
Run pro-life like a profit,

Why should I care about; who-marries-who,
And I'm pretty sure that it,
Shouldn't mean that much to you,

People are obsessed with saying,
"Our religion's better,"
As long as it preaches good,
Why can't they all be treasured?

Why does it matter what Mary-Lee looks like...
Don't you realize condemning her...
Only makes you look more uptight?

Why does it matter, what anybody does?
No more excuses!
"Because, Because, Because,"

I don't really care,
The gossips wrong… and you know it…
So shut your mouth!
Open your mind!
And stop the spread of Bullshit

Jessica Layne Bird 2008

Sadly Few Stand Alone

How many lives have you tarnished,
Because of your hardened rage,
How many lives have you harnessed,
Into your own, inescapable cage,

How many shadows have you cast,
Upon those who could have seen the light,
How many times have you foiled peace,
Just to start yet another fight,

How many tears have you caused,
How many,
Count and see how unlucky,
It is to be the one, who stands,
In the way of the good and justly.

Jessica Layne Bird 2008

The Last Words of the Endless Poet

No, not now, Lord,
A few more years,
My work is not yet done,

I have far too much love, here Lord,
And this life is too much fun,

No not yet Lord,
My body is older,
But my mind and spirit is young,

No, not now Lord,
You cannot have me yet,
My masterpiece has just begun…

Jessica Layne Bird 2008

The Essence of Man

I captured the essence,
The essence of man,
But I threw it away,
As it burnt in my hand!

Evil and lies,
Torture and rape,
Now we burn in our beds,
In which we have made!

No one deserves this,
Not even us,
How could we do this?
To the world that we trust,
How can we hate, our very own people?
Name them words like nigger, loser and cripple!

Not everyone in this world is to blame,
But it's those who are,
Who give us a bad name!
How dare we pretend that nothing is wrong?
As we glorify hate, through words and through song,

How dare we proclaim our love for our God?
When we judge,
Thus stealing,
What is only His job!

How dare we give such names to our humanly brothers!
How dare we feel hate for the children of mothers!
Before you label it,
Think of a child,
Who could be sitting right there...
Would your words be so wild?

How dare we label people?
Especially those, whom we've never meet,
Now who deserves the hating?
Let's make a bet...

I'm not one to complain,
But just one to see the wrong,
So here is just another,
Hate of hate song.

Jessica Layne Bird 2008

Sadness Opera

This darkness is grasping me tightly,
I can't get away,

It's slowly controlling my senses,
My pain is haunting me,

I wish I could forget this pain,
My pain is blinding me,

I can't open my eyes anymore,
I can't take what I see,

So maybe I'll just sleep forever,
It's far too hard to wake now,

They say you have to get better,
If only I knew how…

Jessica Layne Bird 2004

Vice

"I'll kill you," he screamed,
"I'll kill you," she said,
"I'll kill you," the world called,
Bullets to the head!

"I hate you," the child screamed to its own mother,
"I hate you," the stranger called out to no other,
"I hate you," the world called before it found paradise,
Hate was created by men,
What a perfect vice…

Jessica Layne Bird 2008

George Carlin

This here was a man,
Who should have lived forever…
A man of humor, honesty,
And undeniably clever,

His insightfulness,
Matched only by his wit,
A man to tell any force of this world,
"You fucker's are all full of shit!"

Yes, the world will miss George Carlin,
Though his words will still live on,
The world so needed this brilliant man,
To tell the stupid… that they…
…are wrong.

Jessica Layne Bird 2008

Poems of Controversy

Poor Guy

I heard of this one fellow,
His life started out,
A little far from mellow,
A few cries from a shout...

But one day he was given a very big chance...

His father said, "My boy,
You'll lead the country,
Like so many far, before me,
And all you have to do is follow with the dance..."

The poor boy was rather simple,
Not untroubled, to say the least,
But was over- taken,
By his task's power, and romance...

So to the big-house with his family,
His daughters and his lady,
Maybe one day they'd love him,
Like they love that... Armstrong... Lance...

A few years later...

But he made a few mistakes,
And rather big ones too,
And they mocked him,
Even compared him,
To a monkey in a zoo.

But even though I don't agree,
With parts of what he choose to do,
I can't mock when I remember,
"What if it were I who had to choose?"

Jessica Layne Bird 2008

My Religion Rocks!

My religion rocks!
With all the gloom and doom,
I love to hear the wifeless man,
Speak of how God's voice does boom!

And oh, I love those Sundays,
What a Godly fashion show!
All the people showing off their money,
So EVERYONE can know…

Just how godly they are,
So much more Godlier than you,
"I put twenty bucks in the collection plate,
So much more holy than your two! "

Yes, what a fine religion,
Screw evolution, there's virgin births!
A place where we learn Christly acceptance,
As long as they follow, The Verse!

Why should women ever be priests!?
No gay marriage or birth control!
And if you pay us just enough,
Up to heaven you will go!

It's your fault you silly girl,
For one of you ate an apple!
And how dare speak of science!?
Our stanch beliefs will never crackle!

Jessica Layne Bird 2008

Racism Rocks Too!

Racism is good!
Racism is great!
Why should we open our minds?
When it's easier to hate!?

I have a crappy life,
And there's nothing I can do,
So to make myself feel better,
I'm going to blame you!

I don't know you, really...
But I can safely say,
That you're an evil doer,
And all, but my kind, are that way!

Why look at me?
When I can look at you?
And blame you for all the things,
That people like me just couldn't do!

Hey! It says in the bible,
That this and this are wrong!
Did I actually read it?
No... there were no pictures...
And it was kind of long...

But that is half the point!
I know you! Person, I have never met!
And I have lots of bosom buddies,
Who will back me up, I'll bet!

Jessica Layne Bird 2008

I Don't Care That She's Beautiful

I'm about to write a poem,
About someone, who's work I love,
But I just can't agree with something...
Something that she's done...

I have never met her,
And I doubt I ever will,
Though she is rather scary,
Because she's always dressed to kill...

She's the most beautiful woman,
That I have ever seen,
And she's probably the most beautiful one,
That there will ever be.

But I'm sorry pretty lady,
What you did was downright mean,
And your inner beauty faded,
Unlike yours that's to be seen.

I don't care if you're beautiful,
Though, I can't say I blame you,
But what you did those days,
Has done little but to shame you...

Jessica Layne Bird 2008

I Don't Wanna Be In Politics

I don't want to climb,
Up the political latter.
Be on top!? I don't like heights!
And there's just too much useless chatter…

In a political sense,
Being under a ladder,
Is bad luck!
Because if you're not on top of things,
*We'll frankly, you are *ucked!*

Taxes, taxes, taxes for you all!
While the poor are getting poorer!
Though it's not like we'd use that money,
To help them anymore…

Let's use it to build parking lots,
While tearing down apartments,
And now you'll all be homeless,
Because we're raising all the lease rents!

So work another job,
Or two or three or four,
Isn't it just great,
To be the economies whore!

Before people just had to work,
To get their food and rent money,
But now they'll give up anything,
Just to be somebody…

How on earth can the world,
Not care about its people who are here?
Yet we have rallies to save a fetus?!
And signs to slow down for deer!

That's why I don't want to be in politics,
If I had to solve it, I'd go crazy,
And most would not elect someone,
Whose speech wasn't all daisies...

Jessica Layne Bird 2008

Controversial Verses

Controversial verses,
Don't they get some looks?
A great tool for mischief,
Or just to sell some books.

Controversial issues,
They always manage to offend.
Because usually there's an argument,
On either sided end...

But why can't we talk about them?
They are just another issue,
That's really all...

Like talking about the color of shoes,
Or how there are less good stores at the mall,

But the thing behind them,
I'm pretty sure...
Is not the facts; or stats,

Its people's emotions behind them,
And how vividly, they tend to react,
If any of these issues are brought up,
In fact...

Religion, Gay-Marriage, Child-Free, War, Abortion,
Racism, The Nazi's, Economy, and Extortion,
Terrorists, Bombs, Teen Moms, and Public Officials,
Death Penalty, Strip Clubs, Marijuana, Gang Initials.

And these are just a few that I picked,
That seem to make everyone,
Everywhere: sick…

It's really sad that in this world today,
That there are more bad things than good things,
To discuss, and to say…

But maybe if we talked,
And listened about them more,
Without the yelling, the blogs,
And the crying tissues…

Maybe we'd have more subjects,
And a lot less issues…

Jessica Layne Bird 2008

Don't Make Fun of Celebrities...

Don't make fun of Britney Spears,
She's a person too!
She's a mother! You paparazzi...
Shame on you!

Who cares if she shaved her head?
Lots of people do!
Except they didn't grow back,
Gorgeous hair, and make a platinum album,
Or two...

Why does it matter if she gained weight?
Wouldn't you, if you had two babies?
And would you look as awesome,
As she does now?
I'm thinking it's no to maybe...

Don't make fun of celebrities,
Even if it looks like fun,
Because most of them are Americans,
And their rich; and they have guns...

Canadian Celebrities, they are just as bad!
They should dare you Paparazzi Pansies...
To take pictures on our land!
Prove you're not a bunch of Nansies!

Wait outside a Canadian home,
When it's thirty-five below!
Then you'll have earned your little snap-shot,
For all to see, and know!

Jessica Layne Bird 2008

Amusing Almost Sense

The Media Is Nice ©

The media is nice,
It tells us everything!
Like who doesn't like their panties,
And who just pretends to sing!

The media is nice,
Let's ignore everything that matters!
Because it's far more entertaining,
To absorb the mindless banter...

I love all of those segments,
"How to Get Rid of Cellulite!",
Much more important than the world,
Or it's constant hunger fight!

Let's advertise everything,
That will make you fat!
Then once you've eaten it,
Scream out, "Lose Pounds While You Crap©"!

Buy our product now!
You fat tub of lard!
You'll never find true love,
If your abs aren't "Abtron© Hard"!

Let's make the commercials so loud,
That they wake your babies!
"You should have purchased Tro-veg© condoms!",
"With added protection from scabies!"

Everything is for sale, sadly,
Even me and you,
And soon they'll sell our souls as well,
Just wait... and stay tuned...

Jessica Layne Bird 2008

Vampire Books Are Annoying

Vampire books are annoying,
Because they are all the same,
"I've lived centuries long enough,
For me… to finally know,
It's society to blame…"

Wow, we're not impressed Sir Vamp,
Because in your 300 years,
You figured out what most had guessed,
When they were too young for a beer!

You know why few of these books impress,
Because they are written by people!
Fabricating, normal, cookie munching authors,
Who view life as anything but simple.

Vampire books are annoying,
Because people get obsessed!!!
"Let's get our teeth capped,
Then drink some blood…"
This world's getting more messed!

Why does this world,
Make people's lives so bad, or boring,
That their biggest dream in the world,
Is to drink blood, and be pale as Christmas morning?

So let's go out,
Use our real world minds,
Though, it might not be as fun,
Oops, I am a hypocrite,
Cause I too, am writing one…

Jessica Layne Bird 2007

Absolute Nonsense....or is it...?

I'm a hypocrite,
And I don't care,
I'll say it's really ugly,
Then that's what I'll wear,

I'll say that band sucks,
Even though I like it,
I'll say cars; cause global warming,
Though I myself; don't bike it,

I'm a hypocrite and so are you,
Because we are all equal,
Cause everybody poos...

Think about it,
Your nemesis, friends, your boss,
The night before, they ate way too much,
Of that restaurants secret sauce,

So they sit down on the toilet,
Imagine it if you can!
See!
That is why nobody means more,
Than any other man!

We are all equal!
Pass it around!
No one can belittle anyone else,
Because they also flush it down!

And if you have social constipation,
You're not better!
That doesn't count!
Because sooner or later...
You're bullshit will come out!

Jessica Layne Bird 2005

"Anti" People Are Annoying

People are annoying,
Who despise all things commercial,
Because there is something to say to you,
Suzy, Sally and Marcel,

Unless you make your own clothes,
Sheer your own sheep,
And make the fabric,
You're buying something from someone!
Because they wanted you to have it!
...(Even sheep are commercial)...

Buying from the Salvation Army,
That's one good way to beat it...
Except your taking cheap clothes away,
From those who really need it!

But gasp! Those clothes were donated,
Buy people who were consumers,
So you're still commercialized,
But that doesn't mean you're losers,

Going against the grade,
Is a fad in itself!
There's no way you can be different,
From everybody else!

Walk around naked,
Oops, sorry it's been done,
Why don't we all focus on something real?
Once this poem is done,

This poem is also commercial,
For your reading it, aren't you?
And what's so bad with making money,
And doing what you love, too,

Artists sell out for millions…
Don't insult, unless you truly wouldn't too,
Because celebs don't care if someone doesn't like,
That they got paid for… oops, what you couldn't do,

All the way to the bank,
They'll be cut down and called sell-outs,
But who are the real sell-outs here?
The artists or the yell-outs,

"Hey, my friends said that this artist sold out,
So I'm going to hate them,
But I'll secretly buy all their stuff,
Because I secretly like them…"

Why don't we all like what we like?
Regardless of where, or who it came from,
Because if you don't like it, shut up!
It's not like you have to buy some!

Jessica Layne Bird 2008

Metal Music Is Annoying

Hate, death, destruction,
Rawr! Rawr! Rawr!
Blood, Torture, Mutilation,
Blar! Blar! Blar!

I don't fit in to any category,
I sing about things that piss parents off,
I'm here for teenagers to rebel with,
If you don't like it…
@#$% Off! %$#@&*@#$%&%!

I am Metal!!!!!!!!!
And I am ANGRYYYY!!!!!!!!!!!!!!
Insult my fave bands!
I dare you to tempt me….
Grr……………………..

Metal is vaguely annoying,
Though this author does like it,
Though I'm frankly not insulted,
When people don't like it,

It hurts your ears!
Why do we play it so loud?
It's not like there's any old deaf people in the crowd!

We'll maybe there are…
But they are on stage,
The Forefathers of Grrness,
The Masters of Rage…

And if there aren't any deaf people,
Yet… in the crowd,
They'll sure be… next concert,
Because it's so freaking loud!

Jessica Layne Bird 2008

Pop Music is Annoying

Pop is annoying,
It hurts the senses,
Mostly formed of bad lyrics,
And booty shaking dances,

Why are the video girls in belly shirts?
It's winter!
And why does that starlet play football...
In miniskirts?

Why is the new fad,
No underwear... Why?
How much more pants they have to wash,
Must make their maids cry,

Why is it all about,
"We'll there's this boy...",
Or "Sexy, sexy sex...",
Or "I'm rich with lots of toys...",

It can make you sick,
What every song refers to,
But we got to give it one thing,
It's sure fun to dance to...

Jessica Layne Bird 2008

The Vampire Obsession

The Vampire obsession,
The lust for blood and death,
The lust for fearful romance,
An addiction more than meth,

The vampire obsession,
I can see its lure,
A sensuous queen for him,
A forever prince for her,

Imagine a dark lover,
Never to leave you, or to die,
Imagine one, who's near you,
So perfect, you could cry,

Imagine how they'd never,
Fall to what men always are,
They'd never ditch you for their friends,
Come home drunken from the bar,

Imagine, the immortal goddess,
Far too old to complain,
Imagine an ageless beauty,
Her body, by age, unstained,

Powerful, Nobel,
By far, overwhelming,
Look how many books they've been selling,
I can see the industries lure…
Can you…

And after reading this,
Sigh…
I think I want one too.

Jessica Layne Bird 2008

Classical Music Is Annoying

Look at me everyone,
I'm so dapper and smart!
I'm listening to a dead man's,
Last work of art!

You with your silly commercial music poo!
I have, by far, much more culture than you!

I even say poo!
I'm far too classy to swear.
I wear expensive suits,
And read books,
Without nary a care!

I like to show, at any chance,
That I'm smarter than you,
Don't know the difference between Bach and Mozart,
You poor, silly fool!

I guffaw at you!
By the way... that means laugh,
Now go away...
I must ponder my memoirs,
In a chai bubble bath!

...Classical music is annoying,
Because the people who listen to it,
Assume everyone who doesn't is an imbecile...
Yes, that did not rhyme... I know...

Jessica Layne Bird 2008

My Poems Are Annoying

My poems are annoying!
Hahaha! I beat you to it!
Because all I ever do is rhyme,
And complain; about the world's bullshit!

Why do I swear so much?
Do I think is makes me edgy?
It makes me sound like some no brain hick,
Picking at his wedgie.

This book has so many beautiful poems,
With their delightful twists and verbs,
Why did I ever switch to writing the vile?
And the absurd?

Why do I ask questions?
When they're really meant as statements,
When I'm just some white chick,
On her stupid laptop,
In her lonely basement,

God, I complain about everything,
Even if I like it!!!!
Trying to say something through poetry,
And expecting people to buy it?

What a silly fool I am,
I should just quit now,
And I'm insulting myself,
Just to make myself more cool?
"Shut up, stupid self cow!"

I'm a middle class white chick,
With no money problems, really,
Why would I expect anyone to take me seriously?

I came from a tiny, sheltered town…
How dare I write about life?!
And what goes down?!

But hey; the book isn't called,
Eccentric Beauty for nothing,
Eccentric gave me an excuse,
For some real good grumping,

But hopefully out of all,
The annoyance that I spew,
Just one little line,
Will reach out and touch you…
(I meant that poetically,
So stop giggling eww!
What do you know?
That line rhymed too!)

Jessica Layne Bird 2008

C's Poem: To an Old Friend

There once was a girl,
Who'd lost all she knew,
And yet… she was the one,
Who would always come through…

And even though once,
She had lost so much,
To my life, and others,
Her laughter will always touch…

Humble, yet Godly,
The best to be met,
So in this small way…
"I will never forget."

Jessica Layne Bird 2008

To the one person who always got my dry, yet absurd humor.
This one's for you…

Essays of the Eccentric Mind

Contemplation of the Loving Mind
An Essay of Questions

What is love really? Is it contemplated in our minds, and then brought forth in our hearts? Or is it something made up of the soul? Is there really someone who we are meant to be with?

Or do we just happen to stumble upon the person in whom we choose? Are we meant to be with the one we choose? Or do we merely choose the one we do because we find that after love is with us, we cannot give it up?

What if they were existing elsewhere? And you never meet the one you love now? Would it be different? Would you love again? Would you love the same?

Is love an involuntary reaction? To an un-infatuated passion? Are we meant to merely be satisfied with living with someone? Or are we supposed to not want to live without them? Yet if we could not live without, why do so many live to love again?

Can it be love if you are young? Is it a matter of genes? Or a matter of scenes; in which we play over in our minds? And then apply those scenes to whom we seek? Is love memories, or fantasies?

Is it loving to think about the one we love, even when they are not there? But when they are, we have trouble showing that we care? Is it love to want them to be yours forever? But then is it still love, that for their happiness you are willing to let them go?

Love is beautiful, but what pain, and hurt comes with it? Can you love someone so much, that it hurts you... but the pain is worth every minute? Is love supposed to hurt? Should it hurt?

Can you love someone who hurts you? Do you really love yourself if you do? To love you, should they not wish for your happiness? Thus, their hurting of you, would mean that they did not return you love? But can't you hurt someone unintentionally, and still love them?

If it has never hurt you, can it truly be love? Is it love before you can hate the person, but at the same time you would give up everything for their happiness? If there has never been any pain, how do you know its love? If love is painless, then would it wither once it feels pain? Or does pain make it stronger?

Can you love when you are young, inexperienced? And once you have felt love, can it ever leave you? And if love can leave you was it ever really there? Does it matter?

Is love for a person, or are we simply in love with a situation? And if we were in another situation, would we love fuller? Better? Deeper? Or is it that in any situation, you can find a person to love, and love you?

What if you could choose your situation? What if you couldn't? If you and the one you love were in a different situation... would you still love each other? What if you could not be together? Could you still love each other? Is love always enough? If it's not can you love someone, you can't be with?

But if you can give up love, what is love? Was it a chemical imbalance, that later became you heart? Or your heart that caused the chemical imbalance? Or a mixture of the two?

Are we all insane when in love, or is it love that makes us sane? Why is it that the person that can save you from pain, can hurt you the most? What is it about love that makes us trust someone completely with our minds? Our bodies? Our very souls? Even if we shouldn't? Even if we should, but don't want to? If you don't want to love, is it love?

Does love bring happiness, or does happiness bring love? Is it different for everyone? Or do we all love the same? How can you explain a simple feeling? Is that why there have been thousands, millions of songs, ballads and poems written on this under our nose mystery?

Can you ever forget your first love? Is all love based on the first? Do we ever quit loving the past, if all of our futures were grown from it? And if you do not stop loving someone, is that with whom you were meant to be? Are we made to love, since from love we are made? Or is it a choice?

You cannot stop love, yes? You cannot control it? And when you really love, you will not want to leave it? Will it forever exist in your soul, never to be forgotten? Would it be worth the pain of all the knives in the world, once ended, to feel the sweet caress of this emotion for a day?

Should love ever hurt you? Could you ever hurt love? Can love go on and off, like a light, once in white bliss, then in darkness? Can grief of losing love kill you? Or worse kill you soul? Can it kill your mind? Or can your mind kill love?

To hate someone, must you have loved them? If you can know someone enough to truly hate them, is it not like loving them? If those who hated did not hate, would they love one another?

*Is this merely a matter of their situation? In which they choose? Would another situation change that hate to love? Can situations change **true** hate to **true** love? Is there really true hate? Or true love?*

Love like hate; is an obsession is it not? Are the emotions so closely mixed, the pain and the joy? In hate joy is of one's suffering, but in love pain is found in that same suffering.

You can laugh so hard you cry, and cry so hard you laugh. Then why can you not hate and love at once? But hate is wishing pain, and love is wishing joy. In love can you hate yourself and love another? Or must you love yourself in order to love another?

Could you hurt the one, whom the soul that loves you, loves? Could you give that sort of pain to them, having them knowing you are in pain? Or worse? Yet, you would take their pain upon yourself. And yet they would take your pain upon themselves.

Could the wish to follow a lover into death, so as not to live without love, be selfish, or selfless? Is it truly selfish, wishing yourself away from pain? When the one who loved you, would never wish such pain upon you? Must we be a little selfish to love ourselves, and in turn love another?

Is it not easier to give your life for the one you love, then let them do the same for you? Is it not less painful? Therefore is the act of dying for the one you love, selfish, selfless, or merely an instinct to protect ones family? And thus protect ones possible offspring?

Why are those we love taken from us? Why is it that we must live in pain, without our loves? Is it a test of the soul, or are we simply not meant to know the secrets of this world until our death?

Is love over-played? Simply the basis, nay obsession of our society? Or is it something more? Of God,? Or the subconscious? The conscious mind? Why is it that the passions of the mind, will take the place of the passions of the heart?

When you are young, do you love differently than the loves of old? Or with age does love just become more experienced? If you love your first love, and never forget them, why was the first ever ended?

Is love ever really over? Or does it fade into the next life, causing our relentless quest to seek out "the one"? Are we merely ants in the eyes of God? Seen but impossible to hear? Do we die, just to be born again? To continue our relentless quest for the one we have already had? And will have again, and again, until the end of time?

Or is love a choice of our own? Is it even a choice? Is it spoken and shown through a voice? Is it based upon how it's shown? Or does it differ with whom we choose? In love you can have everything to lose. Why do we risk so much for that one feeling?

Why can't we learn to control these emotions? Yet, why would we want to? Is our world so focused on understanding why we love? That we miss out on the simple feeling? Isn't and shouldn't that be why we love? Feeling...

Jessica Layne Bird 2006

Writer's Block

I sit here, staring into the nothingness…waiting.

Waiting…for an idea, a vision.
And perhaps even a nightmare to emerge
from the white depths of this canvas.

Waiting.

Waiting…for just a small extension
of the conscious mind to enter my thoughts.

I'm waiting, for a dream.

Not a dream of sleeping, but of that of the day.
A day dream, a dream to emerge from the emptiness: enter that
    which is my soul, and lead my hand in its creation.

Still my thoughts remain… as nothing.

I look away from the nothing now.
I blindly hope that with my wandering eyes
an inspiration will fall upon me.

Still my thoughts are blank.

I look back, hoping that my creative soul,
will once again take hold!

Still… nothing.

I long for it now, the rush, the passion,
and the sheer power, of creation.

To create a new world.
A world that will be mine.
Mine, to control, to divide… or to bring together.
To create a world of my own!
Be it in beauty, or in pain!

I long for it now, the gentle sound of my pen,
leading its way through my new world.
My pen creating, that which could be the beginning,
or end of time.

Still my thoughts remain blank.

I stare out the window now, and I think of the day.
I consider my life, and I consider the lives of others.
Still, I see nothing but emptiness in front of me.

I stare at the paper now, and slowly I begin to see its worth.
A piece of paper…a small insignificant piece of paper.
What is it to me?

It is nothing!
It is nothing but a thin piece of matter, which somehow came
    into creation and is now, mocking me in my very presence!
I hate it!
This small insignificant piece of paper that began as nothing
is still, just that… nothing!
Yet its sharp edges seem to wound
what it has not yet taken of my creative soul.

I grow angry with it now, as with myself.
It is blank, empty.
There no world, and no story on its surface.
It is nothing!

What if this were another piece of paper,
seemingly identical in every way?
Would it be nothing then?
Would it make a difference?
*Would I then see the story within **its** lines?*
Or would it mock me all the same?

Still my thoughts are blank.

My mind grows numb now, numb to all thought,
numb to all new worlds to be created,
and numb to the fact that this,
this small piece of paper, is worthless.
Yet in its worthlessness… it is priceless in every way…

This flawless white sheet, will decide the future,
the end, and the life, of whatever world
was meant to now be created.

*But still, its lines **still** remain bare!*

I grow angrier now.
So angry…
I lash out!
I stand and I pound my fist against the unwavering spotlessness.

Then…I see it.

I see a small little ripple, a tiny little ripple
in the paper's formerly flawless shape.

I chuckle to myself.
"How could this have angered me so?"
"This insignificant piece of paper…"
"It is nothing!"
"Let its whiteness not be a wall against my will."
"But let it be a beacon of light to create a new world."

A world never heard before!
Never created; until this very moment.
A world all my own; to control.
A world for me, to decide the beginning.
A world for me to decide the end.
And for me to decide what its end will be.

"It is my world," I say to the blank demon,
as it peers back, ignorant to any of its wrong doing.
"It is I who am to blame," I speak aloud.
"My world is not to come from the depths of this paper,
but from the depths of my mind!"
"From the depths of my very soul!"

My thoughts control me now.
My dreaming has begun.

"Shall it be a nightmare?" I ask myself.
"Perhaps a vision of beauty?"
"It does not matter, for the dream is mine."
"Mine alone."
"And this paper does not own my world;
it merely carries it on its back."

My mouth quiets now, and my world waits to lead my hand.
But also, my hand shall lead my world.
Yet the soul controls both.

I stare at the blankness now, no longer in anger,
no longer in shame, but in love and remorse.

This paper, though insignificant and blank,
shall now carry the weight of my world on its shoulders.
Be it beauty, or pain, the burden will be heavy, regardless.
I feel remorse for putting the task
in the hands of something so small, so frail.

But maybe that shall be the task,
for this small slightly rippled white canvas.

It beacons me now, and I sense it is prepared for its burden.
It knows its task, as I know mine.
So I pick up my pen, and begin to write.

Jessica Layne Bird 2007

The Beauty of Eccentrics

The Night Runner

Under the full moon sky,
Snowy footsteps on the road,
One soul amidst the emptiness,
Making their own path as they go...

The street lights they burn out,
As they pass on by,
A dark figure even blacker,
Than the nights own velvet sky,

Run up to the bridge,
To search for something never found,
Whistle with the winds,
As they sweep the icy ground,

Look into the shadows,
Peaceful, and ever calm,
In the silence of the night,
The angels speak their psalms,

Alone, for now and always,
Always to run alone,
Until the day break comith,
And it's time to return home...

Jessica Layne Bird 2009

The People Watcher

She sits there, every day,
She walks there every night,
Studying the faces,
Of those who smile with delight,

Ever intrigued by their joy,
Ever longing for their eyes,
A lonely figure sits there,
A green jacket on her back,

Ever sad, and always alone,
She'll watch them come and go,
But there is just one thing,
This people watcher…
Doesn't know…

Another watcher gazes there,
Watching her, as well,
Wondering why her sadness,
Has caused her eyes to almost well,

Who is this lonely woman,
A green jacket on her back,
And what is her great sadness,
That she must on, look back,

But they would never dare ask,
For as people watching goes,
You watch, you don't approach,
The lives of those that you don't know…

Jessica Layne Bird 2007

The Slow Walker

An odd man walks the sidewalk,
In a new and danceful way,
Moving to his music,
Each step of the way,

Passersby they point, and laugh,
And some just give a look,
Though really there's no harm done,
Nothing, he has took,

He's just a man,
Who moves,
To his own pace,
And rhythm,

And maybe the world would be a better place,
If more would move like him…

Jessica Layne Bird 2008

The Harmless Old Man

The old man, who's forgotten,
How old he truly is,
Or maybe he does know,
But he chooses to live his wish,

He lives throughout this brand new world,
And tries to be, just like the young,
He tries hard not to admire the girls,
Who years ago he may have loved,

Years ago, they would not glare,
Or look at him in fear,
He truly meant no harm,
When he said "You're beautiful, my dear,"

Why has this world's mind gotten so soiled…
That a harmless compliment can be spoiled?

It's sad that as you age, he says,
Remembering his late wife,
How lonely you become,
How you are labeled things countrified.

As a young man,
I could have said whatever I may have wanted,
But I must remember who I am,
And that this is not the life I wanted…

Jessica Layne Bird 2009

The Dog Conversationalist

The old widow woman,
Speaking with her dog,
All the way down the street,
As if it could understand her log,

She'll talk about her life,
Experience past and present,
For the mistakes she's grateful for,
And those that she's resented,

The passersby say to each other,
"She must have a screw missing..."
But she's sane as any one of them,
She's just found someone to listen...

Jessica Layne Bird 2009

The Boomerang Couple

In love again,
Apart again,
Thrown away,
Then taken back,

In love,
Then apart,
Then engaged… forever,

In love,
Happy together for now,
But then, again, the ties are severed…

In love again,
Apart again,
Then in love,
Both with another,

In love again,
Apart again,
And now,
Again,
Together…

But always in love…

Jessica Layne Bird 2009

The Wife with a Crush

The woman with a crush on her husband,
So odd in every way,
So odd for such infatuation to stir,
In a woman of her age,

They've been together for years,
An old boomerang couple of sorts,
But she still hopes he notices,
That she has purchased a new skirt,

She sees him every day,
Yet she still blushes when he looks,
She knows him in every way,
But still scribbles his name on books,

She always wonders why,
This man would be with her,
Why she was picked to be The One,
And not another younger girl,

She watches him as he works,
Outside in the yard,
But she won't dare let him catch her,
She hides her peeking like a scar,

If he ever looks up at her,
As she ogles out the window,
She will pretend to look around,
As if he were nothing but a shadow,

The woman with the forever crush,
Whose love deserves some cheers,
But she won't dare, let him find out...
Though he's known... for many years...

Jessica Layne Bird 2009

Resentment: What We Didn't Choose

The Head-Over-Heels Girl

"I love him oh, so much…"
I said,
"Let's get married next month…"
He said,

It was a love like in,
Some story books I've read,
Except in those, at the end,
They all wound up dead…

"I'm late…"
I said to him, a few months later,
"It's fate…"
Our mother's told all the neighbors,

"Why wait…"
He said, as he gave me that ring,
"You're right!"
I accepted… though I ignored one thing…

And a few weeks later, we heard the wedding bells ring…
I wish I hadn't overlooked… that one simple thing…

"You're late!"
I yelled a few months later,
"I had a meeting,"
He said as he downed a few beers,

"You were supposed to help me, with him!"
I said, my eyes bloodshot and tired,
"It's not up to me…"
He replied,
"I just got fired…"

"You always have excuses!"
I cried, waking the baby,
"It's your job to do this!"
He replied, as he called me lazy...

I was about to reply,
Exactly what I thought,
But it wasn't what I,
Had always been taught...

But the thought it always ran through my mind,
Though it may be selfish, and most unkind...
"I didn't want this..."
"My wish was freedom... and I got this!"

-Miss Taken

Jessica Layne Bird 2008

The Trophy Wife

"Oh, I hope it's a new little brother,"
Stated my husband's overjoyed mother,
"I don't care what it is, I couldn't bother..."
I said dreading who'd be the father,

"Oh, someone is grouchy with morning ills,"
Said the mother, as she inspected my pills,
"You're such a good wife, I hope you know,"
I heard as I wished my head would explode,

"It's such a burden,"
I "wrongly" said,
"It's a miracle!"
She replied, making the bed,

"It's a little soon, for another,"
I said as she left in her truck,
"It's a little late for that,"
She replied as she wished me luck,

I walk into my home,
Clean up my son's mess,
Changed his diaper and bathed him,
And put him "finally" to bed,

I feel the nausea rushing over me,
This is what life is?
It doesn't seem right to me...
Didn't I used to want to be free?

I'm the perfect wife,
And the perfect cook,
But my stress is reflecting,
How everything looks,

It is not longer a fairy tale,
Out of some book,
I wish I had taken the classes,
And lessons that I never took,

I could have been something,
I could have risen above,
But now I am trapped here,
By a "perfect" love…

-Mrs. Trophy Wife

Jessica Layne Bird 2008

The Resentful House-Mother-Wife

Those who "love" me hurt me,
Like no one else can,
Those who "love" me control my life,
The other is a man,

Those who "love" me,
Think they own me,
I'm finally old enough to know,
I only "need" the money,
The rest I "could" let go,

No love for the unwelcome mentors,
Or the students who tie me down,
My love is, was always,
For Freedom,

If I stay here…
Loveless I will drown…

Forget responsibilities?
Forget what I "wanted"?
Hurt those who are without a clue?
Or by this resentment, my regrets…
Till death, be haunted…

"Ding-Dong!"

Oh well... there's the doorbell,
The in laws are coming for dinner,
I'll get the kids washed-up...
Again...
Put on a smile...
For I'm such a "winner"...

-Mrs. Resentment

Jessica Layne Bird 2008

Real Life Resentment

Real life love…
Isn't all it's cracked up to be,
It starts out so blindly,
So infatuatedly,

Real life love,
Sometimes isn't love at all,
Just a once sided relationship,
Where on the woman, it falls,

Real life love,
The woman takes the worst,
Then gives it all, their all,
"Suck it up,"
"You're not the first…"

Real life love,
It will trap you, ruin you, and take you,
Then why would we want it?
Because society will fake you!

The flowery visions of love,
And marriage, and its children,
But everything else!
Is what the stories are missing…

They leave out when he grows old,
And ugly and no longer cares,
And when you're left with nothing,
But forgotten dreams,
And angry tears,

Real love,
The world can have it,
If I'd known before,
I'd be alone…

For all marriage is,
I wish I'd had a clue,
Is a man's excuse…
To spread his name,
And to own you!

Take your real love back world!
I'll live in fantasy!
Because if I dare say something's wrong…
They'll look down on me!

Why didn't someone say it,
That real love will ruin your life,
And you'll give up all your dreams,
To be some oaf's submissive wife,

Children aren't a beauty!
Merely a heart-break and a burden!
But you can never dare let on…
For fear that you might hurt them…

I want out!
I didn't want this…
Godforsaken Step- ford life!
I don't care! Who knows this real love story…
…Of yet another resentful Mother and Wife…

Mrs. Frank Voice of Truth

Jessica Layne Bird 2008

Car Crash

Cars crash,
During a midnight cruise,
Lights flash,
The faint scent of booze,

I was hit dead on,
Front-right corner,
We were crossing the highway,
A wrongly turned corner,

"The other driver was drunk,"
They said,
"An underage, no good punk,"
They said,

"He didn't survive it,"
They said to me,
"You're lucky you're alive,"
They spoke with glee,

But I don't resent that drunken boy,
I resent my driver,
The one who should have looked,
Better, over their shoulder,

I blame you, not that dead boy,
Though they blamed him for it all,
But blame won't let me walk again,
Or halt the tears that fall,

"I didn't choose this…"

Jessica Layne Bird 2009

What Shouldn't Have Been A Bad Thing...

I walk down the street,
My name is John,
My age is ten,
People yell things at me suddenly,
Though I don't even know them,

Why do they call me names?
They don't know me...
We've never talked,
And isn't it ok?
That down this street, I walk?

What's wrong with me?
I feel like my skin is dirty,
I scrub it every day,
Until it starts to hurt me...

It doesn't matter what I do,
I can't get out of this body,
And I'm not sure why it's so bad,
But this is the worst gift God could have got me...

Jessica Layne Bird 2009

At The End

Angel in Disguise

He walked down darkened alleys,
A glimmer in his eyes,
What differed in his presence,
I could not decide,

He moved to me,
Looked upon me,
With no judgments I could find,

He said he knew from long ago,
By this, I was surprised,
He stated everything about me,
From my triumphs,
To my failures,

He said he was an angel,
Born of earth,
Designed by the creator,

As I slowly turned away,
A confused skeptic,
Of his words,
He called that "Not all angels wear silver wings,
And fly about like birds,"

He called that "Angels live on earth,
To help to better things,
Though all must go through hardships,
Before we can fly upon His wings..."

I turned back to face this man,
But he, had left without a goodbye,
So I'll walk the alley ways at night,
To find my angel in disguise...

Jessica Layne Bird 2004

My Guard Angel

My angel will you find me,
My angel, save me from myself,
Will you grant my prayers?
Let me think of something else…

Help me to move on,
From you …
I can't do it alone,
Far too long have I missed you…
Have we both been on our own…

My angel, please help me,
Take it all away,
One more happy memory,
To steal some of my pain,

One more day my angel,
Who was once in disguise,
For when there no longer are alley ways,
I'll forever watch the skies…

Jessica Layne Bird 2009

And She Fades Away...
A Portrait of an Anorexic

Who are you my old friend?
You look so different now.
You have faded so much,
I could hardly tell...

It was you under there,
That mask of skin and bones,
Your heart is breaking,
Fluttering, Failing,
And it will stop before you know...

I worry about you, my friend,
Though I can't help or stop you,
Your killing yourself slowly,
And it's because you want to...

Get help my friend,
You can do it,
I promise you'll get better!

For I live inside you as well,
Don't end our lives forever...

Look at us in the mirror, friend...
We are fading away...
While there are so many,
Who so love us,
And are begging us to stay...

Jessica Layne Bird 2009

Familiar...

I gave the world my strength,
It cast me to the ground,
An enemy I saved,
Before they vowed to bring me down,

I gave all I could to intellect,
And failure it gave back,
I saved one dove from certain death,
As another pecked my back,

I became all that they wanted,
Only to finally know,
That everything they wanted,
Was what I was before,

I gave all that I held dear,
In hopes of something better,
But soon I learned,
What short of time...
It is to last forever,

In life so doomed to give,
And really never get,
In dreams I often wonder,
If my soul had lost a bet,

When young we are lectured,
"You'll be great..."
Just to amount to nothing...

But if I make nothing my goal,
Atleast I'll count for something...

Jessica Layne Bird 2008

Invisible Melodies

As you melodize the streets,
With your invisible guitar,
One day you'll soon become,
The greatest, washed up, faking star,

How truthful the world becomes,
As you display your case of lies,
Until your life is over-come,
With the terrors of your mind,

You walk the street invisible,
With your invisible guitar,
In visible to all,
Though you go unjudged by none,

One heart overflowing,
With the love to never come,
Until you end up mourning,
All you have... that is to come...

So you run to the bridge,
At the time of 3am,
Here the voices screaming,
SO volatile inside your head,

Then you remember those eyes,
And how they're forgetting yours,
You wish to end your life,
Cry out, forsaken and unsure,

But save your breath now,
For the end of your life...you'll need it,
Save your breath for now,
Life's so fragile, you'll need it,

Save your breath for the end of your life,
I promise you, you'll need it,
To say all the things that went unheard,
What your heart was truly bleeding,

So save your breath till the end of your life,
To begin another day,
Save your breath,
For the day, that you have nothing left to say...

Jessica Layne Bird 2008

His Name Was Gabe

An angel came to a woman,
On the Ninth of Ave,
He had some odd advice,
That he wanted her to have,

"You may not know me woman..."
He said,
"But I surely know you,
I know your soul,
I know your mind..."
He paused,
"Perhaps better than you do..."

"I know all of the things,
In which you've long forgot,
I know of a past life,
I know why, it is, you long..."

The woman starred at the angel,
And asked him of his name,
And as he smiled sweetly at her,
He said, "My name is Gabe."

"We'll Gabe," the woman said,
"Why is it that I long?"
"I know because I'm from a place,"
He replied,
"In which you once belonged..."

"That's absurd!" The woman replied,
"No angel am I!"
"You were before your birth,"
He said,
"And once again, when you die..."

Jessica Layne Bird 2007

What Would You Write?

What would you write the last day of your life?
Would you give all the lessons you could?
Or would you thank those you loved,
Forgive those you never would...

Would you list all your regrets?
So they would not be acted by another?
Or would you list all of your accomplishments?
Would you mention yourself... or another?

What would you look back on?
What would wish could be the future?
Or would you even bother to write?
Would you just live the day in a gleeful stupor?

Would tears stain the paper?
Or would your nervousness crinkle its edges?
Would you leave out your faults?
Who would you leave your possessions?

Would writing matter?
On your very last day of life?
Or would you spend it with your husband,
Children, pets, or wife?

I doubt writing would matter,
To very many that day,
Because when death is at your door,
Paper doesn't go a long way...

Jessica Layne Bird 2009

Printed in the United States
146240LV00003B/129/P